PRETEND SOUP

PRETEND SOUP
AND OTHER REAL RECIPES

A COOKBOOK
FOR PRESCHOOLERS & UP

MOLLIE KATZEN
AND ANN HENDERSON

ILLUSTRATED BY MOLLIE KATZEN

TRICYCLE PRESS
BERKELEY

CONVERSIONS

Dry:
¼ cup = 4 tbs = 2 oz = 60 g
1 cup = ½ pound = 8 oz = 250 g

Liquid:
¼ cup = 2 fl oz = 60 ml
1 cup = 8 fl oz = 250 ml

Flour:
1 cup = 4 oz = 125 g

Temperature:
400° F = 200° C = gas mark 6
375° F = 190° C = gas mark 5

Miscellaneous:
2 tbs butter = 1 oz = 2 pats = 30 g
1 inch = 2.5 cm
jack cheese = mild white melting cheese
bell pepper = capsicum
flour = plain flour
zucchini = courgette
baking soda = bicarbonate of soda
powdered sugar = icing sugar
rolled oats = oat flakes
raisins = sultanas
apple sauce = stewed apple
skillet = frying pan

We have taken great care to highlight safety but cannot emphasize too much that anyone working in the kitchen with children must take equal care, as there are potential risks. Neither the authors nor the publisher can assume reponsibility for any accident or misadventrure resulting from the use of this book.

Library of Congress Cataloging-in-Publication Data

Katzen, Mollie, 1950–
    Pretend soup and other real recipes: a cookbook for preschoolers
and up / by Mollie Katzen and Ann Henderson
        p.   cm.
        1. Cookery—Juvenile literature. [1. Cookery.] I. Henderson, Ann.
    II. Title.
    TX652.5.K24   1994
    641.5'123—dc20   93–48579
                                                                            CIP
                                                                            AC

ISBN 978-1-883672-06-5

First Tricycle Press Printing, 1994
Manufactured in China

Cover design by Nancy Austin and Mollie Katzen
Text design by Nancy Austin, Mollie Katzen, and Ann Henderson

18 19 20 21 22 23 – 14 13 12 11 10

Acknowledgments

We are grateful for the wonderful support we received in the creation and production of this book from Nicole Geiger, Nancy Austin, Jackie Wan, Hal Hershey, Carl Shames, Sharilyn Hovind, Toni Tajima, and Cybele Knowles.

Certain teachers and administrators, past and present, of the program for two-year-olds and the preschool at the Child Education Center, helped make this book possible: Darlene Percoats, Gertie Sylvester, Malcolm Waugh, Judith Reich, Rabia Atigee, Tim Herring, Susan Strangeland, Nancy Togami, Mark Hatler, and Beverly Brady. We especially want to thank Larisa Brothers and Laura Brady, who contributed so much to the classroom testing.

A big round of applause goes to the children who so gamely experimented with recipes in the preschool: Marshall Aden, Trevor Bateson, Britt Bender, Christina Berry, Matthew Broadwell, Ellie Buresh, Holly Capell, Tim Clymer, Hannah Ellis, Jessica Feller, Emily Fong, Gregory Friedman, Isaac Gutman-Sparling, Sara Mihich Harden, Katrina Harrar, Connie Harvey, Julia Hendrix, Bonnie and Tommy Hodul, Philip Holub, Anthony Huynh, Noah Isaacs, Daniel and Aron Kingsbook, Ryan Lawrence, Juliana Linder, John Ludwig, Nathan Miller, Jessica Nicely, Erin Pederson, Sara and Sam Pollack, Imogen Poropat, Emma Sarconi, Lee Schneider, Sean Sheridan, Sarah Silbowitz, Mayan Stanton, Amelia Starr, Brittany Thompson, Alice Walton, and Erin Woulfe.

Many thanks to the families and friends who tested recipes at home: Alice and David Walton and Tisha Brewster; Isaac Gutman-Sparling, Gene Sparling, and Marta Gutman; Lynn Hollyer, Amelia Starr, and Gerry Starr; Noah, Josh, Susan, and Larry Isaacs; Hannah and Josh Bishop Moser (with Malcolm Waugh); Angy Stacy and Bonnie, Tommy, Molly, and David Hodul; Chris Tarr and Kevin, Nora, and Madeleine Donahue; Carolyn Kernkamp and Katy, Sarah, Emily, and Bart Fong; Sara Mihich Harden, Sylvia Mihich, and Tom Harden; Sam Katzen Black and Eve Katzen Shames.

We'd like to acknowledge George Young, Lisa and Lou Ekus, David Nussbaum, Anna Erickson, and Leili Eghbal for their enthusiasm and encouragement. Thanks to Betty and Leon Katzen for their thoughtful, helpful ideas. And we send our gratitude to Charles Smolover for suggesting that we name this book after Imogen's comment.

Contents

When my son was in preschool, I would stop by from time to time to see how he was doing. One day I dropped in to discover the children sitting at a low table, intently dicing fresh apples with dinner knives. My son was so absorbed in this task, he barely noticed I was there. The main activity that morning was not about Play-Doh™ or Legos™. It was about homemade (in this case, preschool-made) cinnamon applesauce. The teacher, Ann Henderson, was guiding them and keeping an eye out for their safety, but for the most part, the children were functioning on their own, right down to "reading" the instructions from a pictorial recipe she had prepared. I had rarely seen such a level of interest and concentration on the part of so many small children at one time!

For some reason—I'm not sure why—it hadn't occurred to me to do any cooking with my son beyond letting him watch or stir on occasion. Perhaps I assumed, as many adults do, that three-year-olds are not that interested in preparing food. But then I remembered that by the age of three I had a flat-out passion for cooking—the only difference being that it wasn't with food, but with mud. I used to spend hours out in a mudpile, with my mother's discarded plastic bowls, measuring cups, and spoons, whipping up pancakes and salads for earthworms and snails, and garnishing my creations lavishly with grass, leaves, violets, and dandelions. And now my son and his classmates were cutting apples with the same dedication. The ingredients and the setting were different, but the interest was the same.

Ann told me that she had been cooking with the children every week, with great success. They made—and usually even consumed—all sorts of concoctions, ranging from breakfast foods to blended fruit beverages to soups. Several years later, when my daughter started daycare in the same school, I invited Ann to collaborate with me on a cookbook for preschoolers to use at home with their parents, with recipes that even three-year-olds could follow mostly by themselves. Grown-ups would be the helpers, instead of the other way around. For about a year I went to the preschool every week to cook with Ann and the kids. We also enlisted some families to help out by testing our ideas at home. During this time, we came up with this collection of simple, wholesome recipes that the children not only enjoyed making, but also loved to eat (circumstances which, I have learned, are not always related).

This is the most fun I've ever had writing and illustrating a cookbook! (Many of the drawings contain characters who have populated my personal journals for years.) Collaborating with Ann Henderson has been an absolute delight. She and her students have led me to discover just how interesting real cooking is to very young children. My own appreciation for creative, good food has been enhanced by sharing it on a regular basis with three-, four-, and five-year-olds at the preschool, as well as with my own children, ages two and nine, who participated enthusiastically in the home testing.

Ann and I are both thrilled to get this book out into the world, and to get those little ones and their grown-up helpers cooking up a storm! We hope you and your children have a wonderful time making food together.

Mollie Katzen

Berkeley, California
January 1994

Pretend Soup:
An Owner's Manual

Batter is dripping off a small whisk and down the legs of the kitchen table, but you've never seen your three-year-old so proud. "Ready to eat our muffins that we made?" asks your beaming child. And regardless of the sticky fingers and the state of your kitchen, you can't resist. You sit down and eat together, proclaiming that they are the most special muffins you've ever tasted. And they are, too, because they were made by the excited little chef sitting next to you.

We designed this book precisely for that purpose: to enable very young children to cook as independently as possible under the gentle guidance of an adult "partner." The traditional roles of adult-as-main-cook and child-as-miniature-sidekick are reversed. Your child, as head chef, gets to "read" a pictorial version of a real recipe and do much of the preparation, with you, the attendant grown-up, as helper. Whatever your skill level or background, with this book as your guide, you and your child can have a wonderful time as a kitchen team!

All the recipes for *Pretend Soup* were tested with children—both in the preschool and at home, often with older siblings getting enthusiastically involved. We chose dishes that would not only be enticing, but that could be readily managed by small arms and hands. (For example, the preschoolers loved eating the batch of corn bread we tested, but the batter was too stiff for them to stir by themselves, so we decided not to include the recipe in this book.) And we didn't want to fill the book with recipes for desserts or gimmicky "kid food." Instead, we hoped to get children downright excited about healthy "real" food—food they might not have touched with a ten-foot pole if they hadn't prepared it themselves. Judging from the responses (see "The Critics Rave" section in each recipe), we have accomplished this goal, and we are thrilled!

What is most interesting about cooking to a young child? High up on the list are the tactile experiences, such as kneading and rolling out pizza dough, tearing fresh spinach leaves, or breaking eggs. All the other senses are stimulated, too. It's fun to watch as soup simmers, or a milkshake spins around in a blender, or butter melts in a hot pan. Then there are all the sounds and smells of cooking, and fingers to lick. And usually (but not always), children look forward to sampling the finished product. But what fascinates young children above all is performing those ordinary cooking tasks that we adults take for granted. It's a challenge for little ones to pour milk into a measuring cup, squeeze a lemon, mix a batter, or flip a pancake. Managing these jobs gives them a great sense of accomplishment.

What Do Children Gain from Cooking?

- ✦ A blossoming of creativity and a sense of aesthetics

- ✦ Confidence and self-esteem; a feeling of accomplishment

- ✦ Early math skills (counting, measuring, sequencing of events, an understanding of time)

- ✦ Prereading and beginning reading skills (numeral, symbol, and word recognition; left to right cueing)

- ✦ Small motor skills; hand-eye coordination

- ✦ Strength and endurance (stirring a batter or spreading cream cheese can be hard work if you are only three feet tall!)

- ✦ Science skills (chemistry, temperature, cause and effect)

- ✦ Patience and self-control (waiting for that pizza to come out of the oven is a challenge!)

- ✦ Language skills (observing, describing, predicting outcomes)

- ✦ Ability to follow directions

- ✦ A sense of teamwork

- ✦ Food literacy (an openness to trying new foods; familiarity with fruits, vegetables, other ingredients, techniques, processes—plus a new awareness and appreciation about the foods we eat, what they are, where they come from...etc.)

- ✦ Increased interest and curiosity about all of the above!

How to Use This Book

Each recipe appears twice: first in a conventional format for the adult helper, complete with cooking hints and safety tips; and a second time in a pictorial version for the youngster. Before embarking on a cooking project, read through your section of the recipe first, and take care of any advance setup or food preparation necessary. This will eliminate interruptions once you get started and allow you and your child to concentrate fully on cooking. It will also prevent situations in which you have to leave your child alone with a hot pan while you run off to get a spatula or a pat of butter.

Efficient, experienced adult cooks may have to change gears, slow down, and look at cooking from a kid's point of view. As adults, we often cook to eat, but for children the main event is the process of cooking—not the product. So cook when you are relaxed and have time to really enjoy your child and yourself. These recipes are designed as snacks; they work best if you don't try to make them right at mealtime when your household might be hectic.

If your child is only three or four years old, you will probably want to do most of the food prep and setup by yourself ahead of time. Generally, younger children want to just "do it," while older kids often like to help with everything from grocery shopping to washing dishes. Some children might want to "help" you with the grown-up tasks, but will need your assistance to do so. If you can be patient with this, it will help your child feel useful and important. You can adjust the balance of tasks as the two of you find a rhythm of working together—and of course, this will fluctuate over time as your child grows and gains experience.

Be flexible. If your child doesn't like a particular ingredient or has ideas for improvisation, you can substitute or stray from the written page and have an adventure! And don't worry about precise measurements. For the most part, we have chosen resilient recipes that are hard to mess up.

We all know that children can be picky eaters. Be prepared for yours to refuse to eat some of these recipes, or to want you to eat it instead. There will be other times when they will want the whole batch for themselves! Food waste is a big concern for many grown-ups, and this can set off a

cycle of guilt and tension around food and eating which can have lasting effects. If you can, let go of this concern—we know it's difficult!—and just let your child eat or not without feeling judged. We can help children develop a healthy relationship with food by encouraging them to discover the foods they don't like as well as the ones they do. This will ultimately enable them to know their tastes and eat according to their own appetites, rather than to please someone else.

ABOUT MESSES: Have a sense of humor—don't worry about spills, lumps, or eggshells in the batter. This is all part of the normal experience for the young cook. A child who feels secure about mess-ups will also feel free to keep on trying. There are certain precautions you can take to avoid accidents, however. On the adult recipe pages you will find cooking hints designed to keep the mess to a minimum. At the preschool, we tell the kids that spills are what sponges are for. So keep plenty of sponges around, and a good time will be had by all!

Setting Up

When it comes to cooking, it is neither safe nor satisfactory for your child to stand on a chair or sit on a high stool and work at your level. It's far better to set up a special station, either at the kitchen table or on a child-sized table. Then your young chef can see everything that's going on, and the two of you can sit down together and work side by side. A vertical Plexiglas™ cookbook stand that holds the book open to the recipe is a great help.

Because it is difficult and dangerous for a small child to cook at a full-sized stove, we strongly urge you to invest in an electric skillet that can be used on the tabletop. You will be amazed at the wide range of things you can use an electric skillet for: oatmeal and noodle soup work as well as the more traditional sautéed vegetables, pancakes, or French toast.

A Few Final Thoughts

As your child becomes more attuned to food and cooking, everything that goes on in and around the kitchen will become more interesting, including grocery shopping, setting the table, cleanup, etc. Be prepared for questions about where different foods come from. This might be a good time to look for some picture books about fruits and vegetables, to make field trips to bakeries and farmers' markets, or to plant or visit a garden.

As you cook together, your child will probably want to know more about what's going on and why. Coming up with answers will be both a pleasure and a challenge! In this way, cooking with children can be a wonderful gift for the adult. It reminds us of the miraculous nature of ordinary events—like water boiling or muffins rising—that we often take for granted. If we let it, this partnership with our children can restore a sense of shared magic to our everyday lives.

Safety Tips

✦ Never, ever leave a child alone when cooking! Never leave a child alone in the kitchen when any sharp knives or electric appliances are within reach.

✦ Everyone (adults included) should wash hands before starting.

✦ Short sleeves are best. No one should wear loose clothes that could get caught in food, flames, or the blender.

✦ Keep an easily accessible fire extinguisher in the kitchen, and know how to use it. Use salt or baking soda to put out small flames. If anyone's clothing should catch fire, the rule is: **Stop, drop, and roll! (Children should know this for fire safety in general.)**

✦ Discuss safety in simple, clear terms, especially when a task could be dangerous. For example: "We are turning on the heat now. The pan will get very hot and could burn you if you touch it." Younger children will need frequent reminders.

✦ Keep the handles of pots and pans pointed toward the back of the work area and away from the edge.

✦ Try to do everything at a child-accessible level. (See "Setting up.")

✦ If you are using a regular gas stove, turn off the flame before you stir, turn, or flip the food, then turn it back on when you are finished. If your stove is electric, be sure to warn your child that it will stay hot even after it has been turned off.

✦ Putting things in or taking things out of the oven is for adults only. No exceptions!

✦ About knives: The only knives a child should ever use are serrated dinner knives and strong plastic picnic knives—and only with close supervision. No sharp knives ever!

Cutting is a big challenge for three- and four-year-olds. Let your child practice on Play-Doh™ several times before you move on to real food. It often helps if you guide small hands in a back and forth motion at first. Otherwise, the tendency is to just push down on the knife.

Additional knife safety: Put a piece of colored tape on the handle of the knife. The rule is: Hand stays on the tape. Watch carefully, and remind your child not to slice the fingers that are holding the food. Cut large fruits and vegetables into smaller pieces, then let your child carve further. Use a large, stable cutting board for best results.

Blenders and food processors: It's best to leave these unplugged when not in use. Explain to your child before and during each use that the blades are very sharp and should never be touched. It's okay to let your child push the buttons if you are supervising, but only you should add or remove food from a blender or food processor.

Children's Own Rules

"'GIMME IT' IS NOT THE MAGIC WORD!"

—IMOGEN

"IT'S NOT OKAY IF YOU SPILL ON PURPOSE."

—MATTHEW

"NO HOLDING KNIVES BY THEIR SHARP PART."

—TREVOR

"DON'T PUT YOUR FACE IN THE PAN OR YOU'LL BE BURNED AND YOUR FACE WILL GET AN OWIE."

—JESSICA

"WHEN PEOPLE STIR IT REALLY FAST, THEY START SPILLING."

—JESSICA

"IT'S OKAY TO LICK YOUR FINGERS, BUT NOT THE KNIFE."

—LEE

"DON'T TURN UP THE STOVE TOO HIGH OR ELSE THE FOOD WILL GET TOO HOT."

—LEE

"NEVER TOUCH A COOKIE WHEN IT IS IN THE OVEN."

—NATHAN

"A GOOD RULE IS NO FINGERS IN THE BLENDER."

—AMELIA

"THE MOST IMPORTANT RULE OF ALL IS DON'T COOK IN A VOLCANO."

—NOAH

Quesadillas

The Critics Rave:

"I love them, I love them. They're good, really good!" —LEE

"The cheese looks like frosting. It's melted so it sticks." —KATRINA

"It's so good I would like to do it five times in a row." —NOAH

To the Grown-ups:

Children love eating these as much as making them. Stock up on the ingredients, because when your youngster finds out how good they are and how much fun they are to make, quesadillas may become a daily request for a while.

If you have a favorite recipe for refried beans and you have the time, by all means make your own. The kids will love to help with the mashing. But if you are busy, it's fine to just open a can. There are several good brands of canned refried beans on the supermarket shelves these days.

Children love spreading the beans, sprinkling the cheese (and watching it melt), and flipping with a spatula. In fact, this recipe is an ideal opportunity for flipping practice. Slide the spatula under the quesadilla first, then let your child turn it over. Three- and four-year-olds may need an adult hand to guide them in the flipping.

Portions in this recipe are very flexible. Your youngster might want to skip the beans and just put on lots of cheese instead.

Cooking Hints and Safety Tips (please review pages 11–17):

◆ Older children can help grate the cheese. When we teach the kids how to use a hand grater at the preschool, we talk about how it works, warning about the sharp edges and about how important it is to keep our knuckles out of the way. You may need to guide your child's hand up and down a few times to get started.

- ✦ Use an electric skillet, if possible. This makes the cooking safer, as you can move it down to a more child-accessible level. During the cooking, stay near the pan at all times. If you are using a gas stove, turn the heat off during the flipping, then back on again to cook the second side.

- ✦ The cheese in a freshly cooked quesadilla will be very hot, so be sure your youngster doesn't bite into it right away.

Tools: Tablespoon; dinner knife (for spreading the beans); grater; skillet (preferably electric); spatula; plates for eating; napkins

Quesadilla Recipe

2 tablespoons refried beans

2 six- to eight-inch flour tortillas

a handful of grated jack cheese

1) Spread the beans on 1 tortilla and sprinkle the cheese on top of the beans.

2) Heat the skillet to medium-hot. Place the tortilla on the hot skillet and top with the second tortilla. Cook about 45 seconds, then flip.

3) Cook about 45 seconds on the second side. When it is golden brown on both sides, transfer to a plate.

4) Blow on it until it is cool enough to eat.

5) Eat!

YIELD: **A single portion (easy to make more)**

"The beans and cheese together make it kind of salty. I like that flavor!" —IMOGEN

"It's round because that's how God shaped it, right?" —AMELIA

Quesadillas

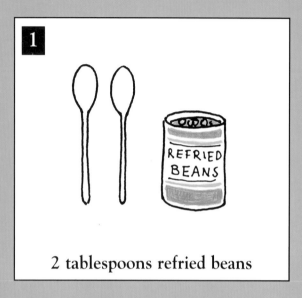

1

2 tablespoons refried beans

2

spread on tortilla

3

sprinkle cheese

4

put another tortilla on top

cook

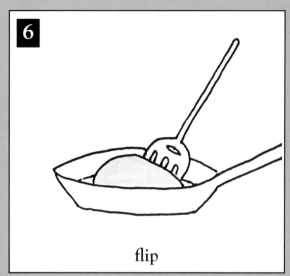

flip

cook on other side

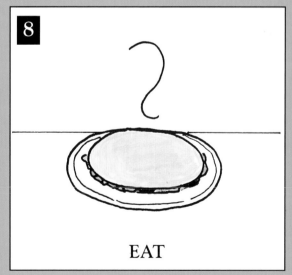

EAT

Bagel Faces

The Critics Rave:

"I'm going to use a big batch of cream cheese." —NATHAN

"This has a happy taste." —EMMA

"I love olives so much, I could eat a whole bunch!" —JESSICA

To the Grown-ups:

Children have lots of fun with this project, which is all about spreading cream cheese (a challenge for little hands!) and creating faces out of various chopped vegetables. In addition to being a cross between art and cooking, it presents a wonderful opportunity to introduce raw vegetables to children, whether or not they choose to eat all of them.

There is no right or wrong way to decorate the bagel. In fact, if your child doesn't feel like making a face, it's fine to make a design instead. Set the vegetables out in separate bowls and let your youngster pick and choose as inspiration occurs. The finished bagel will be just right.

Cooking Hints and Safety Tips (please review pages 11–17):

✦ If you are working with a younger child, do the chopping and slicing yourself and let your youngster wash the vegetables for you. An older child can help you slice the bell pepper (carrots and cucumbers are too difficult). You should cut the pepper into two-inch-wide strips first, then let your child cut slices from that, using a serrated dinner knife—**no sharp knives, ever!**

◆ Whipped cream cheese is easiest to use—let it come to room temperature first for best results. Spreading is harder for small children than you might think, and beginners may need some guidance at first. It helps to tell them to "push down and pull out" with the knife. Remind your youngster to try to cover the entire open side of the bagel, so the decorations will stick better.

Tools: Dinner or butter knives for spreading; small bowls; plate

Bagel Faces Recipe

1 medium-long, thin carrot, sliced into thin rounds
tiny cherry tomatoes, whole or sliced in half
black olives, sliced
1 small bell pepper, any color, thinly sliced
alfalfa sprouts
1 very small cucumber, sliced into thin rounds

OTHER POSSIBILITIES:
    grated carrot (rather than sliced)
    grated beets
    toasted sunflower seeds
    minced chives

1 small container whipped cream cheese
1 or 2 bagels, cut in half

1) Arrange the vegetables in small bowls on a table.

2) Spread cream cheese on the bagel halves.

3) Decorate and eat!

YIELD: Anywhere from 2 to 4 Bagel Faces (or even more, if you have more bagels on hand)

"I love all this stuff!" —ELLIE

"When you eat the sad face, it goes away." —TOMMY

"My bagel's name is Lucy." —AMELIA

Bagel Faces

1

sliced carrot

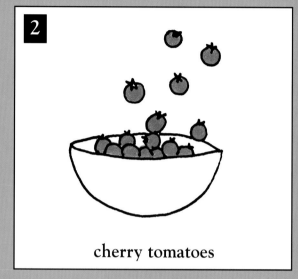

2

cherry tomatoes

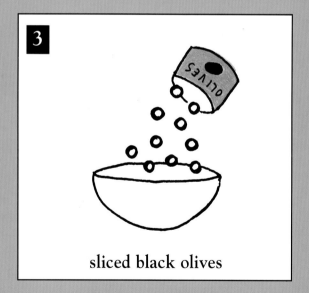

3

sliced black olives

4

sliced bell pepper

alfalfa sprouts

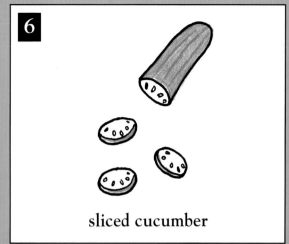

sliced cucumber

MAKE A FACE:

½ bagel

spread cream cheese

decorate

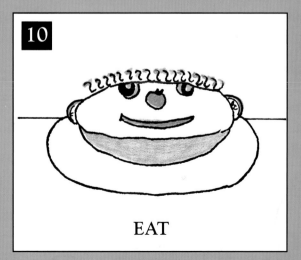

EAT

The Critics Rave:

"They're fat and puffy." —LEE

"Yummy in my tummy! So good, I may eat it all up! That's how good it is." —SARA

"This is so good, I'm going to invite you to my next birthday, but I'm not done eating it yet." —JESSICA

"When you put them in the oven, they grow up." —SAMMY

To the Grown-ups:

The only difficult thing for small children about making popovers is waiting for them to come out of the oven. The batter is simple and light—easy for small arms to stir. Once in the oven, this wimpy-looking batter gets transformed into puffy little breads. Children are amazed by this magic! This is chemistry at its most enjoyable. They'll want to make these again and again.

Cooking Hints and Safety Tips (please review pages 11–17):

✦ The amount of butter is approximate. Let your child cut three pats of butter while you count (or vice versa). Melting it in the microwave is fast and easy. Children love to "paint" the muffin cups with melted butter and may linger over this task for a long time.

✦ A simple way for young kids to crack eggs is to break them on the bottom of a big bowl and let the egg run out into the bowl. It's easier to get shells out of the egg than to get egg off the table.

✦ An easy way to level off flour is to use a ruler. Kids love doing this.

- ✦ To help your child measure the milk, place a one-cup measure in a pie pan. Put the milk in a small pitcher and let your youngster pour it into the cup. Any spills will be contained in the pie pan.

- ✦ Use a bowl that is big enough for enthusiastic mixing. You can help by holding it steady.

- ✦ Putting anything in or taking anything out of an oven is an adult job!

- ✦ When the popovers are ready to be pricked with a fork, have your child wear an oven mitt to protect from the hot steam that may escape.

Tools: Dinner knife for slicing butter; pan or bowl for melting butter; pastry brush; muffin pan (1 dozen capacity); 1-cup measure; ruler; small pitcher; pie pan; mixing bowl; measuring spoons; whisk; ¼-cup measure with a handle; timer; the smallest oven mitt you can find; fork; plates

Popover Recipe

about 2 tablespoons butter

2 eggs

1 cup milk

1 cup flour

¼ teaspoon salt

extra butter, jam, or maple syrup for the popovers

1) Preheat oven to 375°F, and melt butter.

2) Brush the insides of 12 muffin cups with melted butter.

3) Break eggs into the mixing bowl.

4) Add milk and beat well.

5) Add flour and salt and whisk until reasonably well blended—it doesn't have to be perfect.

6) Use a ¼-cup measure with a handle to pour batter into each muffin cup. They should be one-half to two-thirds full.

7) Bake 30 minutes without opening the oven.

8) Remove muffins from the pan and prick with a fork to let the steam escape. Spread with butter and/or jam, and eat! (They also taste great dipped in maple syrup. They're not bad plain, either.)

YIELD: 1 dozen

"I ate a lot of them." —NATHAN

"Can we do this again tomorrow?" —HANNAH

Popovers

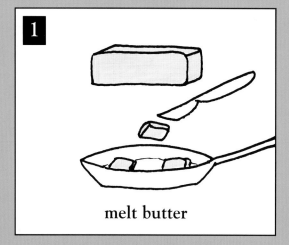

1. melt butter

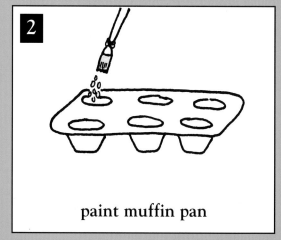

2. paint muffin pan

3. crack 2 eggs into bowl

4. add 1 cup milk

5. whisk

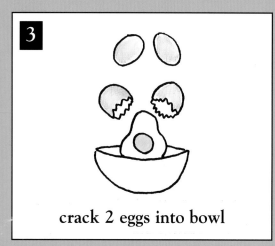

6. add 1 cup flour

7

add ¼ teaspoon salt

8

whisk again

9

fill halfway

10

bake 30 minutes

11

prick with a fork

12

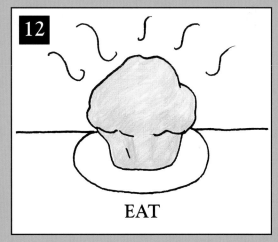

EAT

Green Spaghetti

The Critics Rave:

"I ate all the green spaghetti. I didn't leave any for the other kids." —KATRINA

"Boy, can I smell that! Very good pesto!" —IMOGEN

"Yum! It's good!" —EMILY

To the Grown-ups:

You may not think of pesto as kid food, but they truly love this fragrant, green garlic-basil pasta sauce. The preparation is great fun: they get to pick leaves from a "tree," smash a clove of garlic with a can of soup, and blend it all up.

Fresh basil is easy to grow, even in a limited space, and can be harvested for several months. So consider growing some and plant it early. This way, you can have Green Spaghetti all summer long.

You are in charge of cooking the spaghetti in this recipe, and your child is in charge of the sauce. If you precook the spaghetti and it cools down, you can reheat it easily in the microwave before adding the pesto.

Cooking Hints and Safety Tips (please review pages 11–17):

◆ Children love taking the basil leaves off the stem, but they might be inclined to throw the leaves away, thinking the stem is what goes into the sauce. Remind them to save the leaves and discard the stem.

- A fun way to get the skin off a garlic clove is to put it on a cutting board and let your child smash it with a can of soup. This is effective and very satisfying.

- Oil is hard to measure. It works best if your child holds the empty measuring cup over the food processor and you pour the oil into the cup. When the cup is full, your child can dump the oil into the processor.

- Use a large bowl to mix the spaghetti with the sauce. You can hold it steady as your child stirs, then switch places if more stirring is needed. Stir with forks for best results.

- Be sure to explain to your young cook how the food processor works. Describe how the blades are a special kind of sharp knife, for adults only to handle. Don't let your child attempt to remove the pesto from the machine—do it yourself. Never leave a young child alone when a food processor blade is within reach! It's okay to let your youngster push the buttons, but unplug the machine as soon as you're done.

Tools: Pot for boiling spaghetti; colander; can of soup; cutting board; 1-cup measure; ¼-cup measure; salt and pepper shakers; food processor; rubber spatula; large bowl for the spaghetti; forks for mixing and eating; plates for eating

Green Spaghetti Recipe

about ½ pound uncooked spaghetti

*3 packed cups basil leaves
(about 5 sprigs)*

1 medium-small clove garlic

¼ cup grated Parmesan cheese

¼ cup olive oil

6 shakes salt

3 shakes pepper

a little extra olive oil

a little extra cheese

1) The grown-up begins cooking the spaghetti.

2) Take all the basil leaves off the stems. Discard the stems, and put the leaves into the food processor.

3) Smash and peel the garlic. Add it to the basil, and blend.

4) Add cheese, oil, salt, and pepper, and blend again until it forms a thick paste.

5) Transfer the pesto to a bowlful of hot spaghetti, and mix well with a fork.

6) Optional: Drizzle on a little extra oil, and sprinkle on extra cheese.

7) Put on individual plates, and eat!

NOTE: The salt and pepper are measured in "shakes" to make it easier for the child. This assumes your salt and pepper shakers are not excessively fast!

YIELD: 3 or 4 small servings

Green Spaghetti

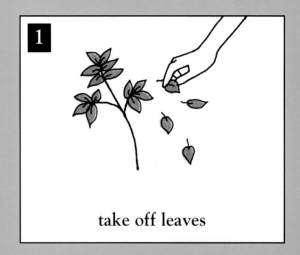

take off leaves

smash and peel garlic

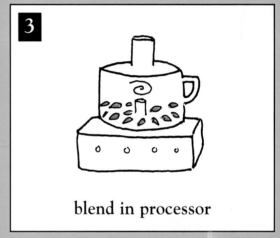

blend in processor

add ¼ cup cheese

add ¼ cup oil

add 6 shakes salt

add 3 shakes pepper

blend again

put on hot spaghetti

stir with a fork

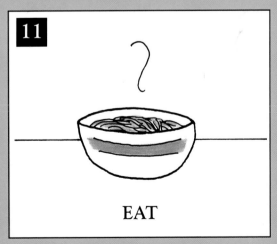

EAT

The Critics Rave:

"I like the berries best." —SARA

"Me too. And I like this stuff and the bananas." —CHRISTINA

"It tastes like ice cream." —RYAN

"While I was eating the soup my tooth fell out." —ERIN

To the Grown-ups:

Even the youngest child can have a great time making this recipe. And if you use fresh-squeezed orange juice—wow! You'll find yourself making it even when you're alone.

Cooking Hints and Safety Tips (please review pages 11–17):

✦ To help a young child measure the juice without fear of spilling, put the measuring cup in a pie pan or a baking pan. Put the juice in a small pitcher, and let your youngster pour it into the measuring cup. If spilling occurs, it goes into the pan, and there is no mess.

✦ Expect honey to be messy. Don't worry too much about exact measurements. Whatever your child can manage will be fine for this recipe.

✦ Use a big bowl for the whisking. You can hold the bowl steady while your young cook whisks away. You can trade places if somebody gets bored or tired.

- ✦ To help a young child peel a banana, cut it in half crosswise, then make a slit all the way down the side of the skin. Repeat on the other side, and give the peel a little tug to start. Then let your young cook do the rest.

- ✦ Another banana note: Bananas are safe for even the youngest child to cut. Use a serrated dinner knife or a plastic picnic knife, and put a piece of tape on the handle so your child remembers which end to hold.

- ✦ If you decide to use fresh-squeezed juice, squeezing the juice will be a fun project unto itself. It is quite challenging for a small child to squeeze juice, so be sure to provide a guiding hand and lots of elbowroom.

Tools: Citrus juicer (if you'll be making fresh juice); large bowl; whisk; small pitcher; pie pan or baking dish; ½-cup measure; 1-cup measure; tablespoon; teaspoon; serrated dinner knife or plastic picnic knife; ladle; soup bowls and spoons

Pretend Soup Recipe

2 cups orange juice

½ cup plain yogurt

1 tablespoon honey

2 teaspoons lemon juice

1 small banana, sliced

1 cup berries (any kind, fresh or frozen; if they're frozen, defrost them first, and use all the juice—it'll add color to the soup)

1) Place the orange juice in a bowl. Add yogurt, honey, and lemon juice.

2) Whisk "until it is all one color."

3) Place 5 banana slices and 2 tablespoons berries in each bowl.

4) Ladle the soup over the berries and bananas. Eat!

NOTE: You can add other kinds of fruit as well. Slices of kiwi are especially pretty.

YIELD: **About 4 servings**

"I like squeezing the orange." —SARA

"I like mixing and doing the berries." —CHRISTINA

"Is this pretend soup? Because it doesn't look like real soup." —IMOGEN

Pretend Soup

put 2 cups orange juice in bowl

add ½ cup yogurt

add 1 tablespoon honey

add 2 teaspoons lemon juice

whisk

add 5 slices banana

add 2 tablespoons berries

ladle soup

EAT

Noodle Pudding

The Critics Rave:

"I can smell it!" —SARAH

"I love cinnamon and I love cottage cheese." —LEE

"The cinnamon is really sweet!" —SARA

"I can't believe I got to eat so much!" —AMELIA

To the Grown-ups:

Basically an unbaked noodle kugel, this dish is simple, nutritious, and filling—comfort food for kids (and grown-ups, too). Try making it for breakfast and serving it with hot cocoa on a winter weekend morning.

Clearly, the big attraction of this dish for preschoolers is the cinnamon. They get to make cinnamon-sugar first in a separate little bowl, and then sprinkle on as much as they want. They love mixing the cinnamon and sugar together and watching the color change.

This dish is a good way to introduce older children to cooking pasta. You can help them observe how the water boils and how the stiff, dry noodles become soft and slippery. Better be prepared to answer questions about it, though.

38

Cooking Hints and Safety Tips (please review pages 11–17):

◆ Please use the utmost caution when supervising a child around boiling water, especially when draining the noodles.

Tools: Small bowl and spoon for mixing the cinnamon-sugar; tablespoon; teaspoon; medium pot for boiling; colander; bowl for mixing; serrated dinner knife or plastic picnic knife for slicing butter; 1-cup measure; forks for mixing and eating; bowls for eating

Noodle Pudding Recipe

1 tablespoon sugar

1 teaspoon cinnamon

½ pound (8 ounces) uncooked flat egg noodles

about 1 teaspoon butter

1 cup cottage cheese

a handful of raisins

1) Put up a medium-sized pot of water to boil.

2) In the meantime, combine the sugar and cinnamon in a small bowl.

3) Cook the noodles until tender. Drain well.

4) Immediately transfer the noodles to a bowl. Add butter and mix well.

5) Add cottage cheese and raisins and mix. (Younger children might need a guiding hand to help them mix. A fork works best.)

6) Transfer to individual serving bowls, sprinkle with cinnamon-sugar, and eat!

NOTE: All amounts are entirely flexible.

YIELD: 3 or 4 small servings

"Mmmmm…good!" —PHILIP

"It tastes like coffeecake." —JULIA

"I thought it was going to be gross, but it turned out to be good." —NATHAN

"I also like cinnamon on broccoli." —NOAH

Noodle Pudding

MAKE CINNAMON-SUGAR:

put 1 tablespoon sugar in bowl

add 1 teaspoon cinnamon

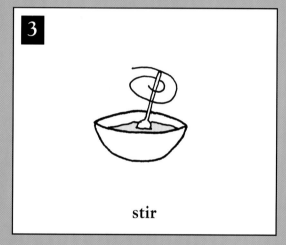

stir

MAKE NOODLES:

cook noodles

put noodles in another bowl

6

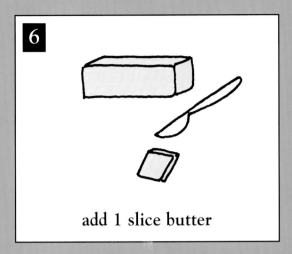

add 1 slice butter

7

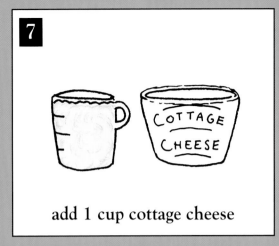

add 1 cup cottage cheese

8

add 1 handful raisins

9

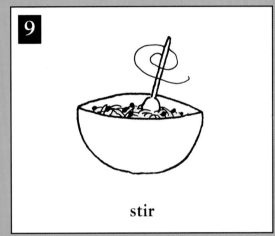

stir

10

sprinkle with cinnamon-sugar

11

EAT

The Critics Rave:

"Can we make another one? Because it's so yummy." —NATHAN

"When you put the butter in the pan, it gets tiny." —SARA

"It tastes like blueberries, like butter, and like syrup." —LEE

To the Grown-ups:

To simplify this rather complicated recipe, you can combine the dry ingredients to make a pancake mix first—then your child gets to make the batter and cook the pancakes. (Don't forget that simple tasks like breaking eggs and beating with a whisk are especially interesting and exciting to young children.)

Five- and six-year-olds might want to help prepare the mix, too, or help wash the berries.

Cooking Hints and Safety Tips (please review pages 11–17):

✦ Here's a great idea to help your child measure the milk: First pour some milk into a small lightweight pitcher with a spout. Put two measuring cups (½ cup and ¼ cup) in a pie pan. Let your child pour into the measuring cups from the pitcher, and if milk spills or runs over, no big deal! It stays in the pie pan. This reduces mess-anxiety on everyone's part and streamlines cleanup.

✦ If you have an electric skillet, by all means use it. This makes the cooking safer because you can put it on a table at a more accessible level.

✦ During the cooking, stay near the pan at all times. Remind younger children that the pan is very hot and they don't want to touch it with their hands. That's why they use the spatula.

✦ Cook one pancake at a time. It's easier for your child to flip it if there is plenty of room in the pan.

◆ When the pancake is ready to turn, loosen it before your child takes over the flipping. Younger children may need you to guide them through the whole process the first few times. If you are using a stove, turn the heat off before flipping, and back on again as soon as you are finished.

Tools: Strainer or colander; small pan for melting butter; 2 medium bowls; pie pan; small pitcher; whisk; wooden spoon; 1/2-cup measure; 1/4-cup measure; small ladle; skillet (preferably electric); serrated dinner or plastic picnic knife; spatula; plates and forks for eating

Blueberry Pancake Recipe

PANCAKE MIX
sift together:
3/4 cup flour
1/2 teaspoon salt
1 tablespoon sugar
1 teaspoon baking powder

1 egg
3/4 cup milk
1 tablespoon melted butter
butter or margarine for the pan
1/2 cup blueberries (more or less)
extra butter for the pancakes
syrup

1) Preliminary: Grown-up combines the mix in a medium-large bowl, melts the butter, and washes or drains the berries.

2) Break the egg into another medium-sized bowl. Add the milk and melted butter, and whisk until well blended.

3) Pour the wet into the dry, and whisk "until you can't see the flour anymore."

4) Heat the pan. Add "1 slice" (1 to 2 teaspoons) butter to the hot pan. (NOTE: Let your child slice the butter. The amount doesn't have to be exact.)

5) Use a plastic 1/2-cup measure with a handle or a ladle with a short handle to pour about 1/2 cup of batter (more or less) into the pan at a time.

6) Place 6 blueberries on top of the pancake.

7) When little bubbles form on the top surface, use the spatula to peek at the bottom. If it is golden brown, that means it's time to flip the pancake over.

8) After the pancake is flipped, wait a minute or two, then peek at the bottom. When it is golden, remove to a plate. Add butter and syrup and eat!

NOTE: You can use frozen berries, defrosted and drained, if berries are out of season.

YIELD: About 6 four-inch pancakes

Blueberry Pancakes

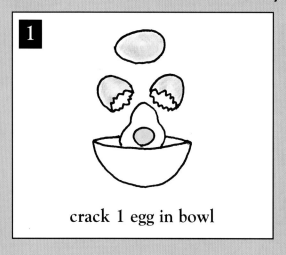

1 crack 1 egg in bowl

2 add ¾ cup milk

3 add 1 tablespoon melted butter

4 whisk

5 pour wet into dry mix

6 whisk again

7

heat pan

8

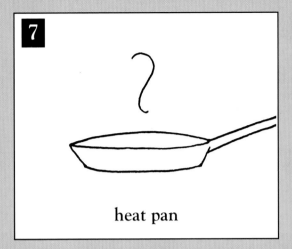

melt 1 slice butter

9

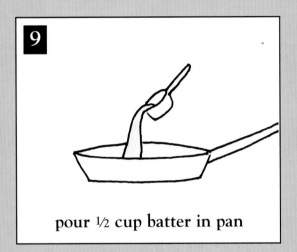

pour ½ cup batter in pan

10

put 6 blueberries on top

11

flip and cook

12

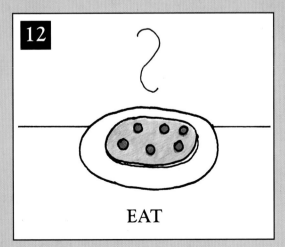

EAT

The Critics Rave:

"My favorite part is the cheese. So I'm eating it." —JULIANA

"It's like a little tiny pizza with salt and pepper on it." —NOAH

"I wish I could have two bunches of them!" —NATHAN *(licking his plate)*

To the Grown-ups:

Zucchini are a popular vegetable among the preschool set. These squash cook quickly, so there isn't a frustrating waiting period between preparation and eating. Zucchini are also relatively easy for small children to cut with an appropriate knife (see next page), if closely supervised. Select your squash according to the age of your child. Experienced five- and six-year-olds can cut a six-inch zucchini, but a three- or four-year-old will have an easier time with a smaller baby zuke. If your youngster has a hard time cutting, try cutting a thin slice lengthwise off each zucchini to keep it from rolling around on the cutting board. If it is still difficult, let your child cut large pieces first, then you can slice them smaller.

Cooking Hints and Safety Tips (please review pages 11–17):

◆ If the children will be cutting, they should use only a serrated dinner knife or a plastic picnic knife. **Never let a child use an adult knife!** Put a piece of colored tape on the handle of the knife to mark the safe end. The rule is: Hand stays on the tape.

◆ Use an electric skillet on a table, if possible, to keep the cooking at a child-safe level.

◆ When the skillet is hot, stay near it at all times. Remind younger children not to touch the pan.

Tools: Child-appropriate knife; cutting board; skillet (preferably electric); long-handled wooden spoon; salt and pepper shakers (make sure they're not too fast); teaspoon; tablespoon; plates and forks for eating

Zucchini Moons Recipe

2 small zucchini

1 teaspoon butter (more or less)

2 tablespoons water

a shake of salt

a shake of pepper

2 teaspoons grated Parmesan cheese (or to taste)

1) Cut the zucchini into rounds about ¼ inch thick.

2) Heat the pan to medium-hot.

3) Put the zucchini, butter, and water in the pan.

4) Shake in some salt and pepper.

5) Stir and cook until it seems done. This will take about 5 minutes.

6) Sprinkle with cheese. (Children love this part! And once the cheese is on, they like to mix it up and smush it around before they settle down to eat it.)

7) Eat! (If it's too hot to eat right away, ask your child to count to 10 while you blow. If it's still too hot, trade jobs and do it again.)

YIELD: 2 or 3 small servings

Zucchini Moons

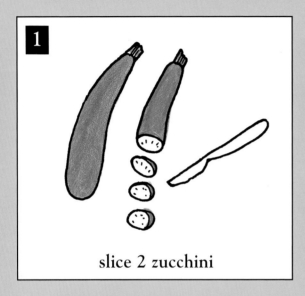

slice 2 zucchini

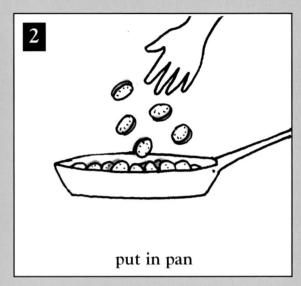

put in pan

add 1 slice butter

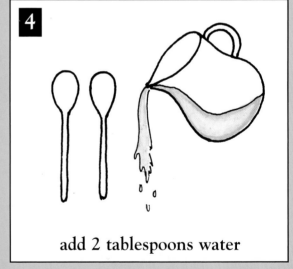

add 2 tablespoons water

add 1 shake salt

add 1 shake pepper

stir and cook

sprinkle cheese

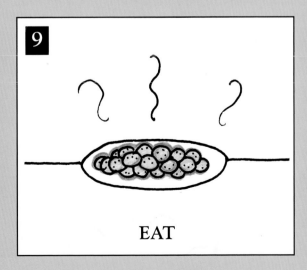

EAT

HOMEMADE
Lemon-
Lime
Soda Pop

The Critics Rave:

"I drinked all of it." —SAMMY

"You know what, guys? Excuse me, it made me burp." —JESSICA

"I like to use a spoon to eat it." —SARAH

To the Grown-ups:

Once the juice is squeezed, the rest goes very fast. Yet even though this recipe is simple, it's still quite an adventure for kids to make their own healthy soda pop, using apple juice concentrate instead of sugar. Don't be surprised if your youngster wants to eat it with a spoon when it's done—it's all part of the fun!

You might not realize how physically challenging it can be for a small child to squeeze lemons and limes. Whatever type of juicer you use, you should supervise the proceedings closely. If you are using the old-fashioned type featured in the picture directions, hold the juicer steady while your child pushes and twists. For maximum leverage, put the juicer on the floor and, while you hold it in place, let your child squeeze from that level. If you don't have a juicer, just cut the lemons and limes into quarters, and have fun squeezing the juice into a large bowl. Strain the results into a pitcher.

Once you've mastered this recipe, you and your child can invent other healthy homemade sodas. Try various citrus combinations—many children actually love the flavor of grapefruit! You can also use other common or exotic fruit juices—fresh, bottled, or frozen. For a special treat, try frozen raspberry, guava, or orange-pineapple juice.

Cooking Hints and Safety Tips (please review pages 11–17):
◆ Cut the fruit yourself and closely supervise the squeezing. Save this recipe for a time when your child's hands are free of cuts or "owies."

Tools: Citrus juicer; strainer; pitcher; tablespoon; ¼-cup measure; 1-cup measure; drinking glass; straw or spoon

Homemade Lemon-Lime Soda Pop Recipe

2 tablespoons fresh lemon juice

1 tablespoon fresh lime juice

¼ cup + 2 tablespoons apple juice concentrate (thawed)

3 ice cubes

1 cup soda water

1) Squeeze juice from a lemon and measure 2 tablespoons into a glass. Squeeze juice from a lime and add 1 tablespoon to the glass.

2) Add everything else and stir. Drink with a straw or slurp from a spoon.

YIELD: 1 serving (easy to make more!)

"I'm a good lemon-lime soda maker. I'm gonna make lemon-lime soda at my house." —HANNAH

"It tastes like the best lemonade in the world." —NOAH

Homemade Lemon-Lime Soda Pop

squeeze a lemon

put 2 tablespoons lemon juice
in a glass

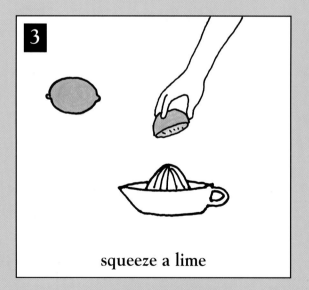

squeeze a lime

add 1 tablespoon lime juice to glass

5

add apple juice concentrate

6

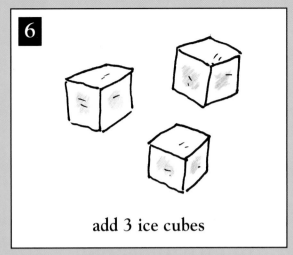

add 3 ice cubes

7

add 1 cup soda water

8

stir

9

DRINK

Number Salad

The Critics Rave:

"I wish I could eat 100 of them!" —MAYAN

"My favorite part is the grapes and the cantaloupes and the bananas." —ELLIE

"I could eat even higher than I can count." —ALICE

"This is not spicy." —JULIA

To the Grown-ups:

This salad, although very simple, is slightly unusual, adding cubes of mild cheese and a light orange-coconut dressing to an otherwise ordinary fruit bowl.

There are really two parts to this recipe: the preparation (cutting fruit and cheese and putting things in bowls) and the assembly (which involves counting out the right number of ingredients). Have patience with your young cook, who may be just learning to count, or too excited to take the time, or not too fond of a particular ingredient—the recipe is definitely open to interpretation. You can make a number salad, too, and let your child help *you* count.

Older children may want to participate in the preparation, including shopping for ingredients and cutting things. If you are working with a three- or four-year-old, prepare the sliced fruit yourself and let your youngster put it into bowls. Your young cook will feel a strong sense of accomplishment simply from assembling this fun dish.

Cooking Hints and Safety Tips (please review pages 11–17):

✦ If your child wants to help with the cutting, use a serrated dinner knife or a plastic picnic knife. Put a piece of tape on the handle so there'll be no confusion over which end to grasp. **Do not let your child use an adult knife!**

Tools: Small bowls for the various ingredients; tablespoon; child-appropriate knife; cutting board; bowls and spoons for mixing and eating

Number Salad Recipe

a handful of toasted coconut

2 tablespoons orange juice concentrate

1 orange, peeled, seeded, and sectioned

1 small apple, sliced

5 dice-sized cubes mild cheese

1 small ripe banana, sliced

*1 small ripe melon—or a section of a larger melon, cut into small pieces
   (you can use cantaloupe, honeydew, or watermelon)*

1 small bunch seedless grapes

1) Cut the fruit and cheese. Put each ingredient into a separate small bowl.

2) Count out the salad ingredients into a bowl.

3) Stir and eat!

NOTE: **If any of these fruits are out of season or hard to find, feel free to substitute and improvise.**

YIELD: 1 or 2 servings (and easily more)

Number Salad

1 handful coconut

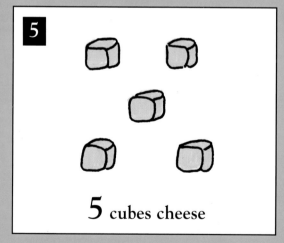

2 tablespoons O.J. concentrate

3 pieces orange

4 slices apple

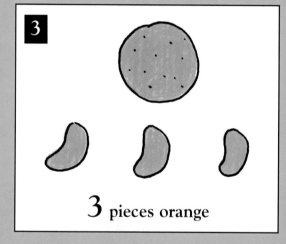

5 cubes cheese

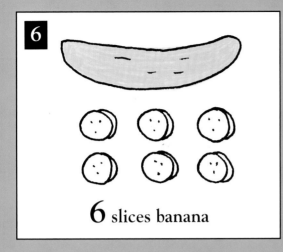

6 slices banana

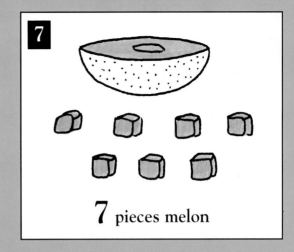

7 pieces melon

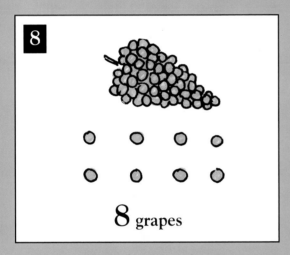

8 grapes

stir **9** times

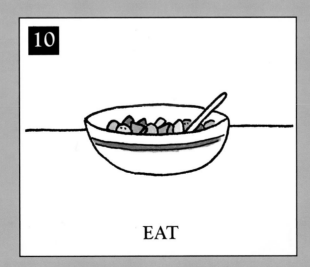

EAT

Noodle Soup

The Critics Rave:

"It's turning into soup!" —CONNIE

"It's bubbling! And the bubbles are really strong, and they're making the stuff move!" —DANIEL

To the Grown-ups:

Everyone loves a good noodle soup, and this recipe teaches children to make a delicious one, starting with dry noodles (as opposed to the already-cooked mushy ones from a can) and fresh vegetables, and without meat or meat-based broth. The most interesting parts of this recipe for the children are preparing the vegetables, watching the water boil, and observing how the noodles soften and the water turns into broth.

This soup contains a small variety of vegetables: mushrooms, which are easy to cut; fresh spinach leaves, which can be torn—rather than cut—into small pieces; peas; and corn. Your youngster can safely participate in every aspect of making the soup. If you are more comfortable cutting the mushrooms yourself, your child can help with everything else.

Cooking Hints and Safety Tips (please review pages 11–17):
✦ The mushrooms can be cut with a serrated dinner knife. Put a piece of tape on the handle and remind your youngster to hold the tape end only. Put the cutting board down at a child-safe height with plenty of room to work. **Never let your child use an adult knife!**

+ Stay beside the pan during the entire cooking process, and remind your youngster not to touch the pan.

+ Be sure the soup has cooled down a little before your child digs in.

Tools: Serrated dinner knife or plastic picnic knife; cutting board; 4 dishes for the vegetables; ¼-cup measure; 1-cup measure; skillet (preferably electric) or a pot; long-handled wooden spoon; timer; ladle; bowls and spoons for eating

Noodle Soup Recipe

1 package ramen soup mix *¼ cup corn (fresh or frozen)*

6 fresh spinach leaves, washed *¼ cup peas (fresh or frozen)*

3 mushrooms *2 cups water*

1) Break up the noodles and put them into the pan.

2) Tear the spinach into bite-size pieces, and slice the mushrooms. Add these to the noodles, along with the corn and the peas.

3) Add the water and the contents of the little envelope of seasoning that comes with the soup mix. Stir.

4) Turn on heat and bring to a boil. Lower heat and let simmer about 8 more minutes.

5) Ladle into bowls, blow on it 20 times, and eat!

NOTE: This recipe uses ramen instant noodle soup mix. The brand we like best is Westbrae, which can be found in most natural food stores. It comes in many interesting flavors that appeal to children.

YIELD: 3 or 4 small servings

"The noodles get soft from the bubbles." —SARA

"A good thing to do is stir it, guys." —ISAAC

"I didn't know it would taste so good!" —TIM

"I just went for that soup!" —TREVOR

Noodle Soup

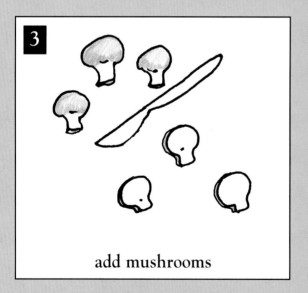

break noodles into pan

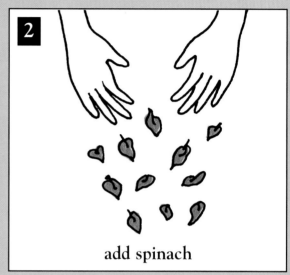

add spinach

add mushrooms

add ¼ cup corn

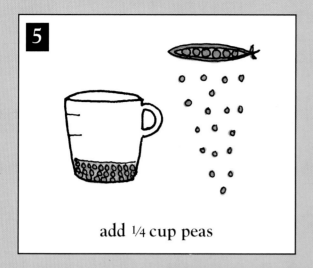

add ¼ cup peas

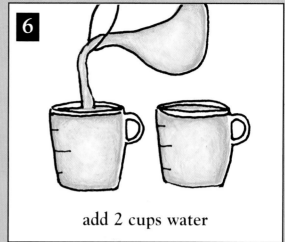

add 2 cups water

add soup mix

cook 10 minutes

EAT

The Critics Rave:

"The vinegar smells really smelly." —ISAAC

"I like dipping the crunchy stuff in the dressing." —ERIN

"I love the dressing. It looks like soup." —BRITTANY

"Thank you for that yummy, yummy salad! It made my arm feel better." —BRITT

To the Grown-ups:

If your child wants to "cook" for the family, this recipe is a good choice.

When we first tried this out with the children in the preschool, it was amazing how enthusiastically they responded! Even the ones whose parents swore they wouldn't go near vegetables just loved the salad bar.

When the children made the dressing, they were pretty sure they wouldn't like it. They were especially uncertain about using vinegar and, in some cases, mayonnaise. But when the dressing appeared at the end of the salad bar, the children seemed to have forgotten their earlier aversions to "smelly vinegar" and "yucky mayonnaise" and went for this transformed substance in a big way! Your child will likely react in kind.

The fun of this recipe is in whisking together the dressing ingredients and assembling the salad. It's best if you prepare the salad ingredients beforehand. Remember that the average preschool cook has an attention span of about twenty minutes on a good day.

Tools: ½-cup measure; tablespoon; ¼-cup measure; medium bowl; small whisk; small ladle; forks and individual salad plates or bowls for eating

Salad Bar Recipe

shredded lettuce (keep the pieces small—child's-mouth-sized)

thin slices of carrot (or you can grate the carrot)

chopped olives

sliced cucumber

grated cheese

cherry tomatoes, sliced in half

a small bowl of toasted sunflower seeds

1 container Chinese crunchy noodles ("chow mein crispy noodles")

croutons

DRESSING

  ½ cup mayonnaise

  3 tablespoons apple cider vinegar

  ¼ cup apple juice

1) Preliminary: Grown-up puts the salad ingredients in bowls or shallow containers, and arranges them in a row on a low table.

2) Put the mayonnaise, vinegar, and apple juice in a medium-sized bowl. Whisk "until it is all one color."

3) Assemble the salad.

4) Add some dressing.

5) Eat!

YIELD: **About 4 servings**

Salad Bar

MAKE DRESSING:

1 put ½ cup mayonnaise in bowl

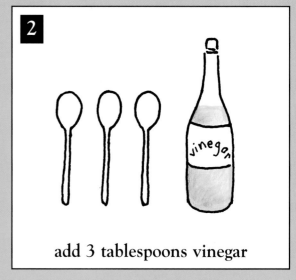

2 add 3 tablespoons vinegar

3 add ¼ cup apple juice

4 whisk

make your own salad

ladle dressing

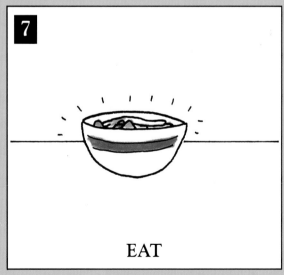

EAT

Carrot Pennies

The Critics Rave:

"The carrots are turning into pennies." —SARA

"I've never had carrots like these before. They're so good, I want more!" —BONNIE

"I can see right through the carrots." —SEAN

To the Grown-ups:

This recipe introduces the young cook to two new concepts: sautéing and making a simple sauce. Your child sautés precooked carrots and glazes them in a sauce of lemon juice, sesame seeds, and brown sugar. Children love the syrup, of course, but they also love the carrots, and it's a nice departure from plain carrot sticks, good as they are.

Cooking Hints and Safety Tips (please review pages 11–17):

♦ Your job is to cut the carrots into thin rounds and precook them either by steaming or boiling. If your child wants to be involved in the advance preparations, scrubbing the carrots is an appropriate task. Cutting, however, requires a sharper knife than preschoolers can safely manage.

♦ When it is time to sauté, let your youngster measure all the ingredients right into the pan before you turn on the heat.

♦ As in all these recipes, it is much better to use an electric skillet than a stove because you can set it at a level where your young cook can work more safely. Stay right by the pan all the time the sauce is cooking, and remind your youngster that it's too hot to touch.

♦ Give your child a long-handled wooden spoon for stirring.

Tools: Child-appropriate knife for slicing butter; salt shaker (of average speed); skillet (preferably electric); long-handled wooden spoon; teaspoon; tablespoon; ¼-cup measure; plates and forks

Carrot Pennies Recipe

2 medium-long, thin carrots, sliced into thin rounds

1 teaspoon butter (more or less)

3 shakes salt

1 squeeze lemon juice (from a small wedge)

1 teaspoon sesame seeds (optional)

1 tablespoon brown sugar (more or less)

¼ cup water (more or less)

1) Preliminary: Grown-up boils or steams carrots until tender but not mushy.

2) Add all ingredients to the pan. Turn the heat to medium.

3) Cook and stir over medium heat until the carrots are nicely coated with syrup. Add more sugar and/or water, depending on how syrupy you like it.

4) Transfer to plates. Blow on it until it is comfortable to eat. Eat!

YIELD: 3 or 4 snack portions

● ● ● ● ● ● ●

"The carrots in the pan are wobbling. The bubbles are like a boat." —SARA

"Do you see that one that's almost like a sun?" —LEE

"Carrots are very good for you, right?" —AMELIA

Carrot Pennies

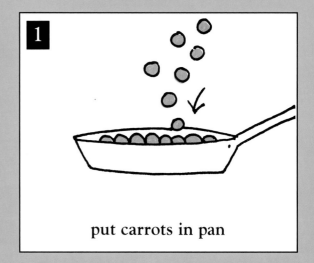

1 put carrots in pan

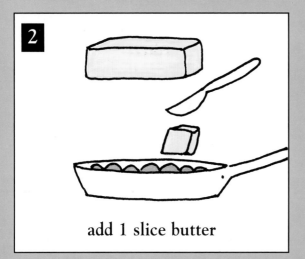

2 add 1 slice butter

3 add 3 shakes salt

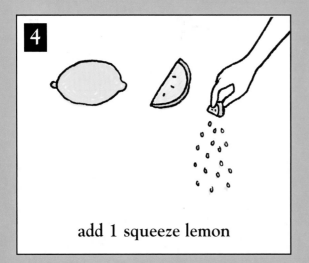

4 add 1 squeeze lemon

5 add 1 teaspoon sesame seeds

6

add 1 tablespoon brown sugar

7

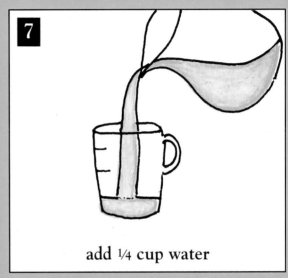

add ¼ cup water

8

stir and cook

9

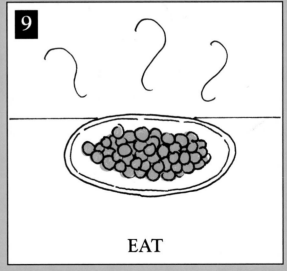

EAT

Hide and Seek Muffins

The Critics Rave:

"Annie, can I have seconds? They are so good!" —SARA

"I'm going to save some for my mom—she loves this!" —MARSHALL

"The strawberry makes the bread good." —JULIANA

"To me, the hiding part is the goodest part." —AMELIA

To the Grown-ups:

Making muffins is a simple enough task for most adults, but for small children, it can be a challenge! Cracking eggs, measuring liquids, stirring a stiff batter, and filling muffin cups are all complex activities to a three- or four-year-old, so to simplify matters, you should prepare the muffin mix and melt the butter first.

The highlight of this recipe for the children is finding the hidden piece of fruit in the center of the muffin. You can vary the recipe by substituting slices of fresh or frozen peach, pitted cherries, or chunks of banana.

Cooking Hints and Safety Tips (please review pages 11–17):

◆ Children love to break the eggs themselves. A foolproof method is to let your youngster crack the eggs on the bottom of the mixing bowl, then just dump the insides in. If you have to remove a few pieces of shell, it's no big deal. Your child will feel quite proud.

◆ Take the worry out of measuring liquids by putting the measuring cup in a pie pan. Let your child pour the milk from a small pitcher into the measuring cup. The pie pan will catch the spills.

- Stirring is hard work. You and your young cook may want to take turns holding the bowl steady while the other mixes. It's fun to count how many stirs each gets. Remember, the batter doesn't have to be perfectly smooth.

- Pouring the batter into the muffin cups is tricky, even for adults. You'll need to hold down the muffin papers and guide your child's hand. Don't worry about the inevitable drips on top of the pan—just wipe them off.

- Putting the muffins into the oven and taking them out are adult jobs! Kids should stay away from the hot oven. Let the muffins cool down before eating.

TOOLS: 1 muffin pan; muffin papers; small pan for melting butter; 2 medium bowls; pie pan; small pitcher; mixing spoon; 1-cup measure; ½-cup measure; measuring spoons; whisk; ¼-cup measure (preferably with a handle), small plate for the extra sugar; timer; toothpick; plates for eating

Hide and Seek Muffin Recipe

MUFFIN MIX
1½ cups flour
2 teaspoons baking powder
½ teaspoon baking soda
½ teaspoon salt
¼ cup sugar

2 eggs
1 cup milk
½ teaspoon vanilla
4 tablespoons melted butter
12 medium-sized strawberries
2 to 3 tablespoons sugar for the
  strawberries

1) Preliminary: Grown-up assembles mix in medium-sized bowl and melts butter.

2) Preheat oven to 375°F. Put muffin papers into the baking pan.

3) Break the eggs into the other bowl.

4) Add the milk, vanilla, and melted butter, and whisk about 20 times.

5) Pour the milk mixture into the flour mixture. Mix with the spoon "until the flour is all gone."

6) Use a ¼-cup measure with a handle to fill the muffin papers halfway.

7) Roll each strawberry in a little sugar, and put one in the center of each muffin, pushing it down with your finger.

8) Bake 15 to 20 minutes, or until a toothpick inserted all the way down comes out clean. Remove from the pan to cool. Cool at least 10 minutes before eating. (The strawberries can get very hot.)

YIELD: 1 dozen exciting muffins

Hide and Seek Muffins

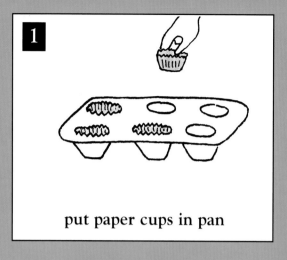

1 put paper cups in pan

2 crack 2 eggs into bowl

3 add 1 cup milk

4 add ½ teaspoon vanilla

5 add ½ stick butter, melted

6 whisk

7 pour wet into dry mix

mix with spoon

fill halfway

roll fruit in sugar

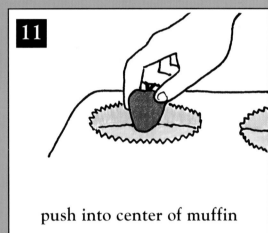

push into center of muffin

bake 15 minutes

EAT

French Toast

The Critics Rave:

"The frying pan is so hot, when you drop something on it, it makes that sound." —DANIEL

"This is so good, I can't even say a word." —MATTHEW

"I wish I could have 261!" —HOLLY

To the Grown-ups:

French toast is so good—and it's even better if you use leftover stale bread. In fact, stale bread is actually preferable to fresh, especially when children are making this, because it is less inclined to fall apart when wet.

Kids like to eat French toast because it's delicious, but they like making it even more because it's a messy, tactile, fun experience. Remember, simple procedures like cracking eggs, whisking, and frying might be commonplace to adults, but they are a very big deal to little children!

Cooking Hints and Safety Tips (please review pages 11–17):

♦ Have your child crack each egg on the bottom of the mixing bowl, then just dump the insides in.

♦ Use a large bowl for whisking together the egg and milk. It provides more stability as well as more elbowroom.

◆ When you are ready to dip the bread, pour the egg mixture into the pie pan. Once the bread gets wet, it's slippery and fragile. Have a spare plate nearby to hold the soaked bread until it's ready to slip onto the hot skillet.

◆ As with all these recipes, it is ideal to use an electric skillet on a low surface (a kitchen table or a child's table), rather than to have the child attempt to reach a full-sized stove. When the skillet is hot, stay near it at all times. Remind children not to touch the pan.

◆ Cook only one or two pieces at a time. If a child wants to do the flipping, be sure you get the bread completely unstuck first and give a helping hand if needed. If you are using a gas stove, turn off the flame before your child flips the French toast. You can turn the heat back on as soon as the bread is turned over.

Tools: Pie pan; large mixing bowl; ½-cup measure; whisk; plate; skillet (preferably electric); child-appropriate knife for cutting butter; spatula; timer; plates and forks for eating

French Toast Recipe

2 eggs

½ cup milk

a pinch (shake) of cinnamon

3 to 4 slices bread (preferably stale challah or sourdough)

about 1 tablespoon butter

optional: syrup, powdered sugar, or orange/raspberry juice concentrate
for the topping

1) Combine the eggs, milk, and cinnamon in a bowl and whisk until well blended. Transfer to a pie pan.

2) Dip both sides of each slice of bread in the batter until well soaked. Transfer to a plate.

3) Heat the skillet. Add about a third of the butter. When it is melted, add 1 or 2 slices of the soaked bread. Cook over medium heat for about 5 minutes, or until nicely browned underneath. Flip and fry on the other side until golden.

4) Transfer it to a plate, add a delicious topping of your choice, and eat!

YIELD: **3 or 4 servings**

French Toast

1 crack 2 eggs into bowl

2 add ½ cup milk

3 add 1 shake cinnamon

4 whisk

5 pour into pie pan

6 dip bread

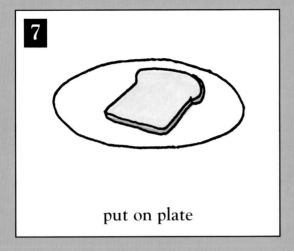

put on plate

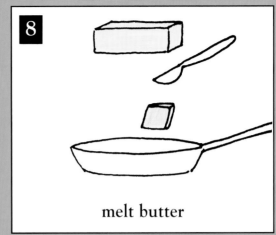

melt butter

put bread in pan

cook 5 minutes

flip and cook

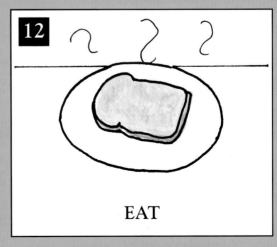

EAT

Oatmeal Surprise

The Critics Rave:

"It's gonna taste yummy!" —MAYAN

"It's going to become bear oatmeal." —ARON

To the Grown-ups:

If this were a science experiment, you would be exploring how heat and water transform dry oatmeal. It is also interesting to watch how the sugar melts on top of the hot cereal. But the best thing about this recipe is that it tastes delicious.

We asked the kids at the preschool why they thought Goldilocks ate that porridge all up. We told them that we had the *actual* recipe, straight from Baby Bear, then we all got busy and found out for ourselves why Goldilocks licked that bowl clean!

Cooking Hints and Safety Tips (please review pages 11–17):

◆ Your young cook will be stirring the oatmeal over the heat. Be sure to use a long-handled wooden spoon. Stay beside the pan during the entire cooking process. Remind younger children not to touch the pan and to stir slowly.

◆ Let the oatmeal cool down before your child eats it All Up.

Tools: 1-cup measure; salt shaker (of moderate speed); ½-cup measure; cinnamon shaker; skillet (preferably electric); long-handled wooden spoon; timer; teaspoon; bowls and spoons for eating

Oatmeal Surprise Recipe

1 cup rolled oats

2 cups water

2 shakes salt

½ cup unsweetened applesauce

a pinch (shake) of cinnamon

a small handful of raisins

a small handful of toasted sunflower seeds

2 to 3 teaspoons brown sugar

milk (optional)

1) Put the oatmeal, water, and salt in the pan.

2) Heat to boiling, then turn the heat down.

3) Stir and cook over low heat for about 5 minutes.

4) Stir in applesauce, cinnamon, raisins, and sunflower seeds.

5) Cook and stir for about 5 minutes more. Transfer to bowls.

6) Sprinkle a little brown sugar on top and watch it melt!

7) Blow on it until it is neither too hot nor too cold, but just right. Pour on a little milk, if you like. Eat!

YIELD: 2 or 3 servings

"It tastes so good, I'm gonna eat it ALL UP!" —JESSICA

"It tastes like an oatmeal cookie. And I like oatmeal cookies!" —EMILY

Oatmeal Surprise

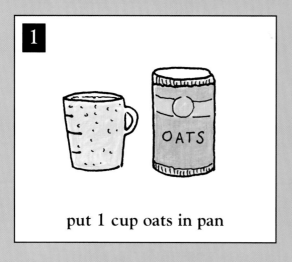

put 1 cup oats in pan

add 2 cups water

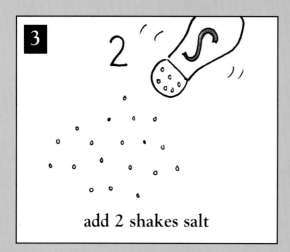

add 2 shakes salt

stir and cook 5 minutes

add ½ cup applesauce

add 1 shake cinnamon

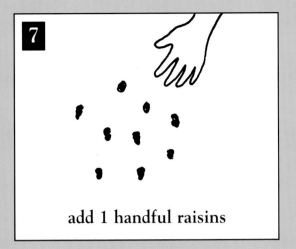

add 1 handful raisins

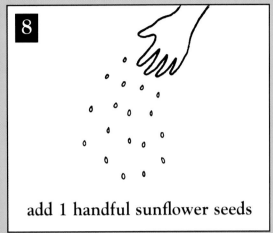

add 1 handful sunflower seeds

stir and cook 5 minutes more

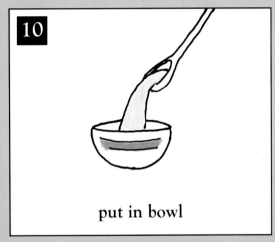

put in bowl

add 1 teaspoon brown sugar

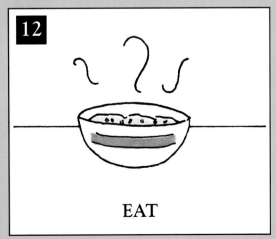

EAT

Chocolate-Banana Shake

The Critics Rave:

"So many bubbles, I can't even count! There might be 177!" —BRITTANY

"It gives you a mustache." —GREGORY

To the Grown-ups:

Once you've made this with your child, you may find yourself making it frequently for yourself as well—it's really good! It tastes like it has ice cream in it—which it doesn't—even when it's made with lowfat milk.

There's very little that could go wrong with this recipe. In fact, it's hard to think of *anything* that could go wrong, unless someone spills the whole thing. Make this on a hot day for a snack, or at lunchtime to wash down peanut butter sandwiches. The main attraction to a small child—in addition to the ritual and delight of consuming the shake—is the process of blending various ingredients into a uniform consistency. Children will be interested to observe how the ice and banana seem to disappear when blended, and how the resulting concoction becomes all bubbly, cold, and thick.

Cooking Hints and Safety Tips (please review pages 11–17):

◆ If your preschooler is struggling with the banana peel, here's a way to make it easy. Cut the banana in half crosswise and make a one-inch slit down the side of the skin. Repeat on the other side. Give the peel a little tug to start, and your child can do the rest.

✦ Closely supervise your child around the blender and be sure to explain that the blades inside it are very sharp. Don't forget to close the blender tightly before turning it on, and unplug it when it's not in use. An adult should always be the one to empty the blender.

Tools: Blender; tablespoon; 1-cup measure; tall drinking glass

Chocolate-Banana Shake Recipe

1 cup milk

½ ripe banana

2 tablespoons sweetened cocoa

3 ice cubes

1) Combine all ingredients in the blender.

2) Cover tightly, and blend until smooth ("until the very loud crunching noise stops").

3) Pour into a tall glass and drink!

YIELD: 1 generous serving (easy to make more)

"It tastes like bananas and like soup." —TIM

"The blender crunches the ice and cuts the bananas and then it gets mushy and chocolaty." —NOAH

Chocolate-Banana Shake

put 1 cup milk in blender

add ½ banana

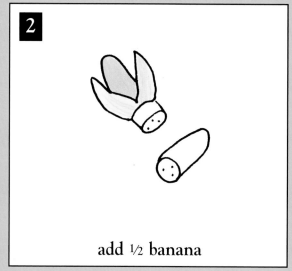

add 2 tablespoons cocoa

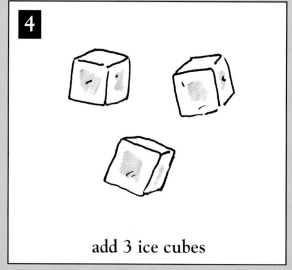

add 3 ice cubes

5

blend

6

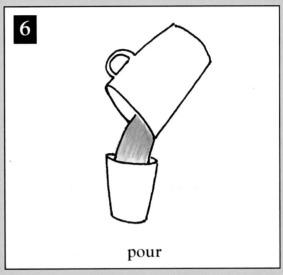

pour

7

DRINK

Pizza!

The Critics Rave:

"The dough feels nice." —HANNAH

"I smell some pizza, dudes!" —NOAH

"Good! Very good! So really very good!" —SAMMY

To the Grown-ups:

Here is a recipe for a real homemade pizza, which can serve to dispel the belief (voiced by several children in the preschool) that pizza comes "from a telephone."

Cooking Hints and Safety Tips (please review pages 11–17):

✦ Bread dough, tactile and sensuous, is very attractive to a young child, especially if you have a miniature rolling pin available for shaping the dough into a pizza crust. A recipe for homemade dough follows the general pizza recipe, but if you prefer, you can use refrigerated biscuit or dinner roll dough from the supermarket. Each biscuit or roll is perfect for an individual preschooler-size pizza, and children can handle this store-bought dough exactly as they would the homemade.

✦ Children like spreading the sauce and sprinkling the cheese on top.

✦ If your child wants to help you grate cheese, be sure to point out that knuckles should be kept away from the sharp edges on the grater. If your child wants to help cut the mushrooms and zucchini, use a serrated dinner knife or a plastic picnic knife (no adult knives ever!) with a piece of tape on the handle to remind the child which end to hold.

✦ Putting anything into or taking anything out of a hot oven is for adults only.

✦ Give the pizza a little time to cool off before serving it to your child.

TOOLS: Wooden board; small rolling pin; ¼-cup measure; grater; child-appropriate knife; baking tray; timer; spatula; plates or napkins (or both)

Pizza! Recipe

½ recipe Homemade Dough
    OR 4 unbaked refrigerator rolls
    or biscuits

oil for baking sheet

flour for rolling out dough

¼ cup tomato sauce

1 very small zucchini, thinly sliced

2 medium-small mushrooms, thinly sliced

¼ cup grated Parmesan cheese

¼ pound mozzarella cheese, grated

1) Preliminary: Grown-up makes pizza dough.

2) Preheat oven to 400°F. Lightly oil a baking tray.

3) Flour a wooden board. For each individual pizza, take a quarter of the dough and roll it out until it is about ¼ inch thick. (NOTE: This is VERY flexible! It really doesn't matter how thick—or even in what shape—the pizza ends up. Your child will proudly love it regardless.) Place on the baking tray.

4) Spread 1 tablespoon tomato sauce over the dough. Add 3 slices of zucchini and 3 slices of mushroom. Sprinkle the top with Parmesan and a small handful of mozzarella.

5) Bake for about 20 minutes, or until brown on the bottom and bubbly on the top.

6) Allow to cool for about 5 minutes, then eat!

NOTE: You can make your own favorite tomato sauce or just buy some premade sauce.

YIELD: 4 tiny pizzas with pizzazz

Homemade Dough

1 teaspoon active dry yeast

½ cup lukewarm water or milk

¼ teaspoon salt

1 tablespoon olive oil

1¼ cups flour

1) Sprinkle the yeast into the water or milk. Let stand 5 minutes.

2) Add salt, oil, and half the flour. Beat for 2 minutes with a wooden spoon.

3) Add remaining flour, stirring, then kneading, as you go. The dough will be soft. Turn out and knead on a floured board for 5 minutes.

4) Oil the bowl, put the dough back in, and let rise for 1 hour.

5) The dough is now ready to use. If you want to store it for a few days, divide it in half, put it in a plastic container with a lid and refrigerate or freeze. Thaw thoroughly before using.

YIELD: Enough for about 8 tiny pizzas (2 batches)

Pizza!

1 sprinkle flour on board

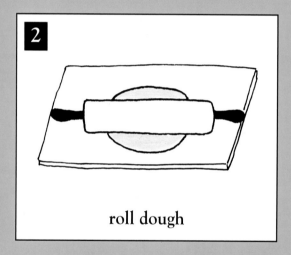

2 roll dough

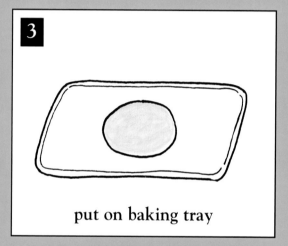

3 put on baking tray

4 add 1 tablespoon tomato sauce

5 spread on dough

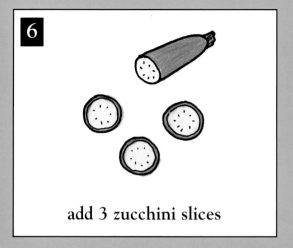

add 3 zucchini slices

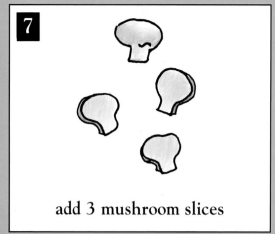

add 3 mushroom slices

sprinkle cheeses

bake 20 minutes

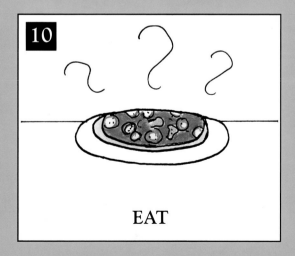

EAT

BRIGHT PINK
Fruit Dip

The Critics Rave:

"It tastes like ice cream." —JOHN

"It tastes like frosting for fruit." —BONNIE

"It gives you a pink face." —ALICE

To the Grown-ups:

This is a very quick and easy recipe—it takes practically no time to assemble, even if you are working with a three-year-old. It's a good choice for a day when your youngster needs some practically-instant gratification. When we tested it in the preschool, the kids were licking their bowls, their fingers, and other people's bowls—it was a big hit!

Kids are always fascinated by what goes on in a blender. Before you turn the blender on, ask your youngster to guess what color the dip will be when it's done. Afterwards, you might be asked *why* it turns pink, so be ready with an explanation of some sort.

Cooking Hints and Safety Tips (please review pages 11–17):

✦ This is a rich raspberry-yogurt dip that you scoop up with spears of fruit. The emphasis for the child is on puréeing the dip ingredients. The grown-up (possibly with the help of older siblings) prepares the fruit for scooping. Plan ahead to make this dish by remembering to defrost the raspberries.

✦ For some reason, frozen *sweetened* raspberries (packed in a ten-ounce box) seem to work better in this recipe than either fresh or frozen unsweetened. If you like, you can explain to your child that raspberries actually grow outside on bushes, not in frozen food departments, but that they sometimes get picked, sweetened, and frozen to be sold in stores.

♦ Explain to your child in simple language how a blender or a food processor works, and that fingers should never, ever go inside the container. It helps to tell kids that the blade is a special kind of knife that is very sharp and must be touched only by adults.

♦ Kids like to push the blender buttons, and this is okay if you are right by their side and if you keep the machine unplugged when not in use. **Remember: Using a blender or a food processor should always be a closely supervised activity!**

Tools: Blender or food processor; child-appropriate knife; rubber spatula; mixing bowl; whisk; serving bowl(s); serving plate(s); napkins

Bright Pink Fruit Dip Recipe

spears of cantaloupe or honeydew

spears of fresh, firm banana

apple or pear slices

FOR THE DIP

1 ten-ounce package sweetened raspberries, defrosted

½ cup (4 ounces) softened cream cheese

1 cup firm yogurt

2 teaspoons lemon juice

1) Arrange spears of fruit on a small plate.

2) Place the raspberries (including all their liquid) and cream cheese in a blender or food processor, and purée until uniform. Transfer to a bowl.

3) Add yogurt and lemon juice, and whisk "until it is all one color."

4) Pour the dip into one or more serving bowls. Dip the fruit spears into the pink stuff, put your face over the bowl, and pop the fruit right into your mouth!

NOTE: This recipe calls for frozen sweetened raspberries. If you are using fresh raspberries or frozen unsweetened, add about 2 or 3 tablespoons sugar or honey (to taste).

YIELD: 4 or 5 filling snack portions

"Mine tastes like flowers." —AMELIA

"This tastes so good, I'm going to take a long time eating it." —BONNIE

Bright Pink
Fruit Dip

1

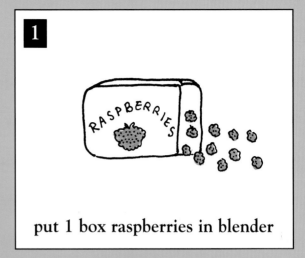

put 1 box raspberries in blender

2

add cream cheese

3

blend

4

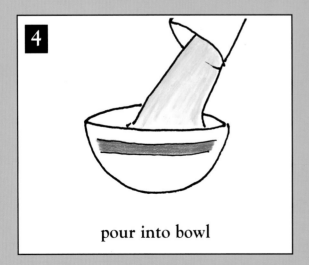

pour into bowl

5

add 1 cup yogurt

6

add 2 teaspoons lemon juice

7

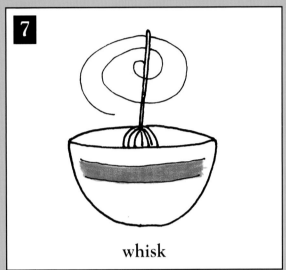

whisk

8

serve with fruit

9

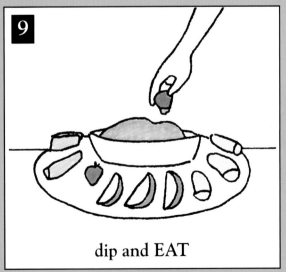

dip and EAT

A Few Other Ideas

*Here are some suggestions for quick and simple treats you and your child
can make together with little or no advance preparation or planning:*

✦ PEANUT BUTTER SANDWICHES

Even though peanut butter sandwiches are everyday fare, children still find it a novelty and a challenge to spread the peanut butter themselves. If you have soft bread, toast it first, then put it on a plate or a cutting board. Remind your young cook to "push down and pull out" while spreading. Serve open-faced, decorated with raisins, fresh peach slices, banana slices, or grapes.

✦ TEA PARTY!

This is a favorite: a play tea party with real food! Try peppermint tea sweetened with a little honey, and jam-on-graham-cracker teacakes. Make the tea about ten minutes ahead of time to give it a chance to cool down. (You can hurry this along by adding a few ice cubes.) Let your child fix the teacakes. If you use a smooth topping like apple butter or unsweetened fruit spread (available in natural food stores), your child can easily spread it on the graham crackers with the back of a spoon. A child-size tea set will make everything truly elegant. You and your child can serve each other.

✦ CINNAMON TOAST

This is the classic snack for a rainy day or at bedtime. Children love to make cinnamon-sugar, sprinkle it onto hot, buttered toast, and watch it melt. Add one tablespoon sugar to one teaspoon cinnamon in a small bowl, and let your child stir it "until it is all one color." Put the toaster at child level, and let your youngster put in the bread and push down the lever. (With a toaster oven, your child can close the door and push the button.) Supervise this activity closely! Explain that, other than pushing the buttons, we never touch the toaster—it is very hot! Let your child use a dinner knife or plastic picnic knife to spread the toast with softened butter, then sprinkle on the cinnamon-sugar with a spoon. Do everything on a big plate, and cleanup is easy!

✦ FRUIT JUICE POPS

Let your child pour fruit juice—any kind—from a small pitcher into miniature paper cups, and freeze them. (Put the cups on a pie pan to catch the spills.) The eating procedure involves licking the top, then gradually peeling off the paper. (Children will instinctively know how to do this.) For an added surprise, put a small piece of fruit in the cup before pouring the juice.

Suggested combinations: orange juice with a slice of banana or a strawberry; lemonade with a raspberry or blueberry; apple juice with a slice of peeled peach or apricot.

✦ BANANA POPS

Here's a good use for those really ripe bananas that you can't quite bring yourself to throw away. Peel them and place them in a large bowl. Let your child have a great time mashing them with a potato masher, then transfer the purée into miniature paper cups, and freeze them (same idea as in the Fruit Juice Pops).

✦ POPCORN

Making popcorn is an exciting ritual for small children, who love the sound, the smell, and sometimes even the short but tantalizing wait until it's ready. In this age of microwaves, it is a special treat to make popcorn in a hot-air popper or a skillet popper with a glass top so children can see what's happening inside. Let your child measure the ingredients (use a pie pan to catch spills), and make sure to hover close by, reminding the young cook not to touch the hot container during the popping process. Other fun tasks for kids include slicing the butter to be melted, pouring the melted butter on top, and dispensing the salt (be sure your salt shaker is not too fast!).

✦ FRESH-SQUEEZED ORANGE JUICE

If you have an electric citrus juicer, this can be a wonderful project for you and your child. (Remember that what often seems so obvious to us adults can look like a big adventure to a three- or four-year-old!) You can include an excursion to the market to buy the oranges, and maybe even talk about where oranges come from and how they grow. Don't let your child cut the oranges—this is strictly an adult job! However, your budding chef can safely and effectively help with the squeezing and pouring, if closely supervised. Use a pie pan to catch any spills, and be sure your child's hands are free of any open cuts before you embark on this project. Fresh-squeezed orange juice is especially cheery on gloomy days.

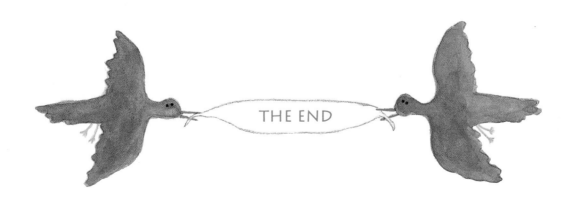

THE END

MOLLIE KATZEN, a charter member of the Harvard Nutrition Roundtable, is the author/illustrator of the celebrated cook book trilogy that includes *Moosewood Cookbook*, *The Enchanted Broccoli Forest*, and *Still Life with Menu*, as well as *Vegetable Heaven*. Her second cookbook for children, *Honest Pretzels*, was recently published by Tricycle Press. Her cooking show appears on public television stations nationwide. Visit Mollie's web site at www.molliekatzen.com. She lives near Berkeley, California with her husband, son, and daughter.

ANN HENDERSON began her career in education as a summer camp counselor and art director. She is an early childhood education specialist and is the director of preschool programs at the Child Education Center in Berkeley, California. Over the past ten years she has cooked more with her preschoolers at school than she has at home. When she is not cooking or teaching, Ann collects and restores antique bubble gum machines and Central American carved wood and tin religious art from the early 1900s.

SPECIAL OFFER TO EDUCATORS:

Tricycle Press has produced an educational supplement to PRETEND SOUP—and it's free! Learn how to set up a cooking program at your school, how to incorporate cooking into your lesson plans, and how to have a great time doing it.

Visit the "Educators" section of our Web site, www.tenspeed.com, to download the teachers' guide.

MORE CHILDREN'S COOKBOOKS BY MOLLIE KATZEN

Salad People
Honest Pretzels

TRICYCLE PRESS
BERKELEY
WWW.CROWNPUBLISHING.COM
WWW.TRICYCLEPRESS.COM